GYPSY SONG

GYPSY SONG

Poems by

Deming Holleran

*For Susan —
In the delight of words —
Deming
July, 2015*

Antrim House
Simsbury, Connecticut

Library of Congress Control Number: 2014952621

ISBN: 978-1-936482-76-4

First Edition, 2014

Printed & bound by Mira Publishing, Inc.

Book design by Rennie McQuilkin

Front cover artwork by Portia Fitzhugh

Author photograph by Mim Adkins

Antrim House
860.217.0023
AntrimHouse@comcast.net
www.AntrimHouseBooks.com
21 Goodrich Road, Simsbury, CT 06070

For Romer
intuitive reader of my poems
and steadfast mate
in the adventure of life.

ACKNOWLEDGEMENTS

The following publications first issued poems contained in this volume, often in earlier forms:

Iodine Poetry Magazine: "Her Sextant" (as "To Call on Stars")

Main Street Rag: "Into the Mist"

The Breath of Parted Lips: Voices from The Robert Frost Place, Volume II: "Trash Day"

The Still Puddle Poets: "Her Sextant" (as "To Call on Stars"), "Summer Lights," "Into the Mist," "Summer's Fog"

The Still Puddle Poets – New Poems: "In Florida, After You Left," "Listen to Your Heart," "Back in Gstaad" (as "Last Night in Gstaad"), "Coming Out"

Profuse appreciation and gratitude are offered to:

Pamela Harrison, source of my initial efforts at writing poetry, who has held my hand through the journey as an astute, generous and inspired reader and as a true friend who has pushed me to the limits of discomfort (including making me take a ballet class) in order to bring me to deeper levels of emotional engagement.

Phyllis Katz, friend and mentor, and all the rest of the Still Puddle Poets, past and present, whose familiar voices have provided many years of poetic camaraderie and generous critiquing.

My friends, teachers and fellow participants at The Frost Place, who have labored mightily to help me improve my art and craft.

And to my husband and children, who have all embraced my poetic self as though she were part of me all along.

TABLE OF CONTENTS

VI. LISTEN TO YOUR HEART

AT THE FROST PLACE

You will cross a river, the first metaphor each day,
and you will think how many sources
feed the waters, and how many more
will join them from the greening hills; how some
trickle, others gush, and many gather force
within the slopes before they stream –
like words from poets' pens.

You will climb the dusty road to the old
dilapidated house and writers' barn, its doors
flung open in embrace, and all the milling faces
will be new. You may think yourself a child
at the aquarium, beguiled by all the shapes
and curious ways of fishes, and ache because
your wish is to be one of them.

You will mimic how they glide through words
in effortless suspension, while a see-through wall
still hems you off, 'til one soft morning while reading
your new poem to someone on the lawn, you'll hear
a camera's shutter click, and looking up you'll cast
a self-effacing poet's smile toward the tourist van below,
and know that you belong.

I. WHAT WAS GIVEN

COMPANIONS

When I reach back to lift the shroud
cloaking childhood memories,
the shapes of trees loom closer than the rest,
rooted in the place I knew as home.
Parents and older siblings drove, sailed, flew
away like skittish birds to far-off lands,
while nurses, maids and cooks changed faces
and I attached to none.
The trees, though, held their ground,
and stretched their branches out
like arms of welcome and embrace.

Two rows of stately pines along the drive
stood guard like sentinels, whispering
among themselves as wind blew gently
through their boughs, which lifted up
like giant wings outstretched against the sky,
and overlapped the passage
to the place my parents named "Still Pond."

Around a bend, just as the house came into view,
dividing lawns from deeper meadow grass,
huge islands of forsythia grew, fortresses
for me to crawl through beneath the tangled sprays.
There I stowed my treasures: smooth stones, feathers
or a robin's egg. Some days I sat cross-legged,
an Indian waiting out the cavalry attack,
and whittled sticks for arrows by the score.

Behind the house, wisteria blossoms hung from ropes
of twisted vine, thicker than the muscled thighs

of circus strongmen, and there I climbed and swung
like Tarzan in the perfumed jungle,
surrounded by a symphony of bees.

By the far-off pond, a weeping willow
hovered over ducklings at her trunk,
like a disheveled spinster aunt.
Her pliant sprigs became my lariats and lassoes
for driving thirst-parched cattle
to drink from the shimmering water hole.
If I hungered from the herding,
a tidy apple orchard grew beyond the pond,
offering juicy fruit, rosy polka-dots
on crinolines of green.

One tree blazed brighter than the rest,
in every hue of red and gold and orange,
a maple in the sheep-field where the ram,
mean-spirited with snorts and corkscrew horns,
threatened my approach. Like sacred fire
defended by a dragon, that tree beckoned me,
the fifty yards from fence to bottom branch
an epic quest. Rewarded when I scrambled up
and safely nestled in the lap of limbs, I was
amazed to find the leaves glowed green within,
as at the center of a torch's light,
while farther out they burned, a ring of flame
protecting me.

                Curious companions,
those trees that comforted my early years

and tower in the mind. Eventually they died,
cut down or rotted, every one, made way
for others, just as people do, leaving
in their wake occasional stumps to mark
the passing of their lives, gravestones
in my memory's burial ground.

MONTGOMERY

I spent my childhood springtimes
on an island in a southern sea.
There, along its azure shore,
grew scrubby trees dangling
thick, round, shiny leaves
that lovers etched with their initials.
Once, I too took a sharpened twig
and carved a heart enclosing a rough *M.*

Back then, scraggly sheep and chickens
eked out life before becoming dinner,
and four sturdy burros trudged the uphill path
laden with leather suitcases,
food, and five-gallon jugs of water.

Early mornings before their day's work,
the island boys and I would ride those steeds
across the salt flat, pursuing bandits
out beyond the ruins of an ancient sugar mill.
My mount was white like the Lone Ranger's,
taller than the others, with wise brown globes of eyes
and a soft gray-whiskered muzzle
that puckered up when he grabbed
my breakfast sandwich, wax paper envelope and all,
and slowly gnawed it with his big square teeth.
His bristled mane grew helter-skelter,
barely long enough for me to clutch while lurching
side to side upon his bony spine,
his quick short burro steps
a full gallop in my mind, and I
leading the posse out to rout the outlaw band.

That I should love a burro
named for some brave general
did not seem odd, and so
I asked the grownups
if we could marry, he and I.
They told me yes, and promised us
the spit of land called Monkey Point
for wedding gift. The matter might
have been forgotten, as burros
were replaced by jeeps and
romances of a different sort
but one year,
barely out of childhood, I found again
the leaf that bore a heart and M –
now welted scars cracked brown
and barely legible, and remembered
how a girl once thought a donkey
would make the perfect mate.

THE ROAD HOME

The darkened limbs of oaks hulk overhead
along the lonely roadside where the child,
a Christmas Pageant angel homeward bound,
grasps sticks to guard against the dread
of shadows, while imagination, wild
and fearful, conjures reasons to condone
abandonment. Why weren't they there, when all
the other children's parents came to call
for them, proclaiming gladly what a fine
production it had been, how proud they were
of their own shepherd, Mary, Joseph, king
or angel. Tired, cold, forlorn, but there
at last, she eyes their tight and merry knot:
it is the cocktail hour, and they forgot.

WHAT WAS GIVEN

was two mothers:
one at birth,
the other unfolding
like a rose to the child
who ventured to her door.
Aunt Helen,
with milk and cookies,
two kitchen chairs
and time to talk.

LILI

Every year, the same card. Alice, in white
and black with small red bow, staring
in wonder at a Christmas tree, musing
for one word to mean so much.

How many cards had Lili ordered, thousands?
Or did she special order them each year? What
meaning did Christmas hold for Lili, childless,
to prize this wonder in a child?

She confided there had been a botched abortion.
It left her womb barren. Wartime it had been,
and Phil away. A lone trip to a back street clinic.
She, who loved the person in each child,

would never know her own.

What were the swirling sentiments in the air
when she was at our home? Something of
mystery to a child, something of sex. I learned
much later she had bedded my father's brothers

and maybe my father. What was she to a child
but wonder, a presence who stirred the air, put
my mother on her guard. Spell-master with
stories, seductive. High cheekbones, raven

hair and deep black eyes that sparkled. Lili,
who dressed only in black and white.

BY THE CHIMNEY WITH CARE

That year, Santa Claus delivered.
Perhaps because – on Christmas Eve, after
all the relatives drove off, when
I had scrubbed dark lipstick kisses
from my cheeks, and Grandpa's cigar-smell
was fading from the velvet dress
whose starched lace cuffs and collar
now lay rumpled on the floor,
I called my mother in to say
goodnight, and help me
hang my stocking.
"What could I leave for Santa?" I asked,
thinking sugar cookies, ribbon candy, milk.
"Scotch," she said,
"that's what he really likes. I'll fetch
a bottle from the bar."

                    We left it
on the firegrate with a small note signed
Love…
                    By morning, it was gone –
in its place, a bulging stocking,
          and the key to Santa's heart.

DADDY SHUM

My daughter asks, "What was he like,
my grandfather?"
Efficiently, I proceed directly
to the tidy reference catalogue
of my mind, where I keep
my memories in neat compartments.
With practiced concision, I respond:
"Just under six feet tall,
great sense of humor, cameras always slung
around his neck, organic gardener,
an avid fisherman, a modest man."
Curiosity thwarted, you drop the subject.

Help me! Take my hand
as I took yours
when you were small,
lead me on tiptoe
past that beartrap mind
into the neglected forest
of my senses.
Ask again.

Each time I taste a crust of fresh-baked bread
he's there –
slicing off the end from one of four dark loaves
steeping the kitchen with the rich aroma
of his latest inspiration: molasses, wheat germ, honey,
and asking, very seriously, for my opinion.

When I smell the acrid tang that hangs in photo shops,
I'm bathed with him again in ultraviolet light,
a wide-eyed child prodding chemical solutions
with wooden tongs, helping him perform the darkroom magic,
changing spectral sheets of blank white paper
into photographs still hanging in our home.

The sight of anglers casting line
into a swiftly flowing stream
recalls the way he taught me:
"Raise the rod to two o'clock,
while counting one-chimpanzee-two,
then let it rip!" And his would sail
uncurling through the air, to lightly drop
the fly exactly where a salmon's rise
had roiled the water just before.

Now the sound of neighbors raking leaves,
scratching muffled rhythms in the earth,
returns me to his side. Khaki-clad, an old fedora
shielding his bald pate from sun, he'd sweep
enormous heaps for me to leap into, and I'd fly
fearless from the roof of the clucking chicken coop,
he chuckling with pride.

The feel of him returns
when you and I are wrestling
playfully, unequal in our strength
since you are nearly grown and I am growing
older. When I was small enough
to crawl into his lap and pester him

to roughhouse, he twisted me
into contorted pretzel shapes,
then I would squeal delight,
and beg for more.

So, my dear, ask
and ask again –
spring my beartrap mind.

BACK IN GSTAAD

Scents of barley soup and garlic spew
from my hotel's kitchen, thick as
syllables of Schweizerdeutsch, savorous
with memory. Inside, checkered curtains
framing lace-cloaked windows; outside,
the muffled sound of shovels scrabbling
at snow-mounds where a three-day-blizzard
deep-cushions the restaurant's hush. The portrait
of a sole geranium stares down from a wall.
Alone at one of fourteen tables, and sated
with wine and veal in cream sauce, I scribble
on the tab images from two teenage years
plus twenty weeklong winter stays with mother
and my growing girls. Today I breathed in
the cow-dung pungence from weathered barns
along the winding street that wraps itself
around the mountain's flank, then passed
by Charley's Tearoom, where I learned
to smoke and danced with dark-eyed boys
who may have ended up as kings, and mumbled
Grüssi to the godlike ski instructor of my youth,
who now walks with a cane.

SIGI'S WORLD

Somesville, Maine

Bright speckled hens bob
clucking among the ferns,
one matron gazing motionless,
glass-eyed, toward the brood –
wood-carved, un-feathered she,
a trick, an *amuse-bouche*
for the senses' palate
before the feast, the breath-catching,
eye-ravishing feast of my friend's home.
A slender copper pipe drips
slow melodies into an enormous
moss-greened urn; the pebbled path
waits stripe-raked for the doe to set
her hoof-prints, like notes
on a musical score. At dawn the aroma
of coffee and bacon lures me
from scented linen sheets to join Sigi
at the sea-side table on her deck.

Here somehow the bald eagle knows
to choose this moment for its sweep
across Somes Sound, as later
in the morning does the starfish,
bright and knobby-spined, when it glides
into the smooth gray-pebbled shallows
shadowed by my legs. Who could blame

my asking Sigi if she had lent a hand
when, on the sheep-white, shaggy runway
of my bedroom rug a dragonfly alights,
its double wings of light-spun gossamer
spread wide, emerald head sparkling,
one antenna folded gently above its eyes.

II. INTO THE MIST

SUMMER'S FOG

I cannot recall what started
the argument that has left the small vein
on your forehead pulsing like a timepiece,
measuring our silence.
Fog cuts across the long potato field
in front of your parents' cottage, isolating
the sun-blazed yard with its plastic
striped folding picnic chairs, pale blue
hydrangea bush and split-rail fence
from the sea-view beyond.
You flip through a magazine, focus on a picture
of a whale, breaching, hold it up it to me,
a reaching out. The fog is creeping
toward us, an immeasurable pillow
suffocating even the oak trees,
even the profligate bunch roses growing
along the fence. In minutes, your mother
will shuffle through the door on metal canes,
her high-seated chair borne by your father.
A frenetic gray mole skirts the porch steps
and dives into a hole near where we sit
in fraying red wicker chairs that came with the house,
half a century ago. Soon, the necessary conversations.
After cocktails, dinner, at precisely seven.

FAMILY VASE

How suddenly it shattered,
heirloom bearing memory
of mother-art passed on:

generations of women gathering stalks,
setting them at angles, blooms
trumpeting beauty's jubilant display;

emblem of the home, fractured
in a careless sweep of hand,
bruised petals strewn among the shards.

Just so, love splinters at the hasty word,
but seamless to the eye, mends up
with fault lines where the reckless rifts have torn.

INHERITED CLOCK

For years you drowsed upon the weekly-dusted shelf,
gazing on the world – a tarnished face entombed
in a splintering wooden case, the key to your internal life
long lost – legacy from a dear departed friend.

Attuned to VPR, my ear perked up at word of a master
reputed to bring back the souls
(and bodies) of dead clocks.

Half a year you spent in that magician's shop,
eventually returned, transmuted, faced
with sparkling silver in a field of burnished brass.
Delicately fashioned hands of curling steel
kept staunchly their appointed rounds,
and, most miraculous of all, your voice
made hourly pronouncements in clarion tone
above a constant rhythmic beat. A striking presence,
you perched more purposefully there.

Grown accustomed to your now persistent pulse,
one day I sensed a faltering, faint arrhythmic murmur.
Bewildered as the fibrillation worsened,
I summoned your physician.
"Just a minor problem, not to worry,"
he declared; "I'll have to take her to the shop though,
for a while." A while became three months
of unmarked time.

At last returned with ticker steady
and facelift holding up quite well, capriciously
on the first day you gained ten minutes,
the next day chimed six strokes at five,
then twenty-one at twelve!
I think I'd better stop the clockworks here
before your hijinks get too queer.

MY MOTHER CLIMBS THE STAIRCASE

to be read from bottom right

obtains elusive summit, straightens up triumphant, and smiles.
of purposeful resolve, 'til finally her wasted frame
grip exhaustion clamps on every advancing fiber
A baleful, draining sigh betrays the obdurate
obstinate habit more than rational aim.
following its groaning mate, obeying
and nearly threadbare will; foot falters,
could ease the burden of worn joints
a quavering hold on air
splays fingers forth as though
alabaster hand
in creaks and moans,
banister
vie with
Bones

ELDERGAME

I know the game that older people play,
communally agreed upon – a way
to circumnavigate a common word
and make the exercise look less than absurd.
Yet it takes decorum and etiquette
to know which type of words one can forget.
The skill lies in artfully concealing
the momentary lapse by revealing
some curious or thought-provoking feature
of that mislaid name or thing or creature
(you know – our friend who almost went insane
after her daughter ran off with a Dane.)

So why last night did it chill me right through
when you couldn't recall exactly who
was *that horrible man in World War II?*

INTO THE MIST

Fog shawls the islands' shoulders
and the silent river, where a loon call
lingers in the early morning light.
My mother lies in the cool bedroom
of her house of fifty summers.
She is nearly eighty-eight, and weary,
opening her clouded eyes on one more day.
I see her head propped on pillows,
folds of skin thinner than the faded
collar of her nightgown. We are alone
and she asks, "Where am I?"
I cannot answer. I do not really know.
Her voice, my mother's voice, is high,
as hollow as the loon's. She leans
toward me, stretching hands like
sparrow talons searching for a perch.
My hands meet hers, and I am pulled down,
down into the mist, into the pillowed
cloudbank and the withered scent of her,
and I answer from the only place
that matters now, "You are with me."

BAFFLEMENT

How can you have forgotten
that you love to dance
the Charleston, that you paint

bright trees and beaches, and
stitch a needlepoint pillow
for each grandchild? If

you're no longer she who dances,
paints and stitches flowers,
who are you? And do I

love you now that you're no longer
you, or do I merely care
that you be cared for?

I too was helpless once.
You made sure that I was tended,
fed, dressed, diapered.

I'll do the same for you –
not personally of course –
that's quid pro quo.

KEEPING THE WATCH

In my mother's room
      the air weighs   heavy
with spirits
      waiting
           beckoning
while she murmurs
      "Help me, please help me"
and we
      I and my sisters
don't know how.

We light
      three candles
play tapes – Celtic harps
          and hammered dulcimers
to help ourselves.

She mumbles one word
      for two long days
          before we understand
"Charlie"
      and summon him
          fellow gambler
but more importantly
          a man.

He chatters on
      self-conscious in her

absent   presence
then leaving
touches her, says
"Goodbye, baby."

That night   at last
she quiets

and is gone.

III. MUSINGS

FANTASY OF TWO GARTER SNAKES
IN SPRING

New York Botanical Gardens

She glided by one sunlight-dappled afternoon,
all undulant and graceful, flashing crisp stripes
of dazzling ochre on a field of deepest olive –
what to do but follow? Past the murmuring runnel,
faster through the sprouting rock garden, faces
of viola, leukojum, anemone all bowed low,
and up, up, up onto a matted thatch of soft
cotoneaster. The new green growth mingling
with last year's crackling leaves of gold made
camouflage, and there we lay, our bodies
easing into one another's need, braiding
ourselves in delectable slowness, motionless
but for the occasional twitch by our farthest reaches,
her head resting lightly where my body curled,
as the wind whispered *spring* to the cherry trees,
and a shower of petals wafted through the air.

SVELTE

She will wake
craving cucumbers
laced with dill
(rather than French toast),
will place her feet
on the floor,
feel ankle bones
meet, knees too,
no calves between.
In the mirror,
Modigliani
not Rubens
will gaze back
and the watchband
will slacken at her wrist.
Hip bones will rise,
twin gentle hills
beneath her gown.

In town, slender
strangers' smiles,
complicit. Jeans
of different cuts
beckon, for
the fun of trying on.
Passing by
store windows,
she'll steal
sly glances

at her reflection,
admiring its lines.
Seatbelts on a plane
will need tightening,
her queensize stockings
will have to be replaced.

HARBOR BEAT

Key West

They keep it upbeat
down at the pier – reggae
pulsing, lunchers' toes
tapping out the rhythm
on sun-bleached planks,
pastel umbrellas swaying
lightly with the breeze,
bikini babes and gay guys
in tight white jeans swinging
lissome hips while sipping
mango cocktails by the bar.

I even caught a steel crane
halfway across the harbor,
slow-dancing, sultry.
She raised her dredging arm
and dipped, as though
in presentation, turned
a swivel in the air,
and cocked her wrist,
coquettish, then dropped
a showering spray of sand,
like a handkerchief of lace.

AT THE NATATORIUM

We pause at the end of the pool,
synchronous after ten or twelve laps.
Catching our breath. He wonders –
don't I think that swimmers should be
handicapped for foot length, just as
jockeys are, to equalize their weight?
The idea has merit, I must agree,
looking down through aquatic distortions
at his size 14 feet, and considering
this might indeed explain why
he completes every length
seconds sooner than I, then waits.
Not that we compete.
Still, one can't help noticing.
He pushes off again,
bubbles trailing in his wake
like small quixotic musings of his mind.

LEARNING POLISH FROM SZYMBORSKA

This much I've learned from a dual-language edition
after giving my eyes blanket permission
to wander leftward to the Polish lines
and try to decipher word meanings or rhymes.
Ki and *ach* denote plurals of nouns,
and *wszystko* means *everything,* I've found.

How evenly the English word can dispense
packages of vowels and consonants
in alternation – e.g., the lovely *hepatica*
(which Szymborska renders *przylaszczka.*)

If poetry is music, could words like these
sound lyrical to Polish ears?
Psy are dogs, and only one's a *psem,*
but how you would pronounce them
is anybody's guess.
Imagine this:
a Polish scrabble set, with *i*'s and *e*'s
as rarities, and *x*'s as commonplace as *z*'s!

Consonants parade across the lines unshamed
by almost exclusive association with the same
type of folk as they –
but isn't that the way
with humankind?
In any culture, like-minded seeks like mind.

FAN MAIL

My name is Julie and I work at Social Security processing
Change of Address requests. I am hoping I have the right Dem-
ing. It seems I do since the Yahoo address for you matches the
request you sent to Social Security. You did not send us your SSN
so it is not possible to change your address as requested. I could
call you if I had your phone and get your SSN that way or you
can resend your request to us via mail with your SSN. Please ad-
vise. I also love your poem Into the Mist. I can relate to this poem
since my father is frail now at 83 and it is hard to accept this.

Blessed be the serendipity that sent my letter
        to your inbox, Julie;
blessed, too, my oversight in failing to include
an SSN in my request.
I see you at your carrel up on the seventeenth floor
of a gray-beige concrete government high-rise,
computer screen in front of you,
        a pile of correspondence to the side,
a picture of your parents on their honeymoon,
        pinned to the left wall.
They look young and smiling and hopeful, waving
        from a ferry boat
which may be taking them to see Niagara Falls,
        up close inside the mist.

Blessed be their birthday gift when you turned ten,
        a trilogy of Nancy Drew,
that fired your imagination to play the sleuth
        as life presented chances,
and modeled perseverance to pursue a lead
        until you find an answer.
Blessed even be the resource of Yahoo

for bringing my poem to you,
where it managed to provide a bit of consolation
as you watch your father fail.
Blessed be the quirky ways two people ever
get connected.

LIVE OAK

Outside the gray glass second-story window
of the Vero Beach Public Library, a great live oak
spreads twisting boughs like punch-drunk pythons
dancing to the music of the breeze. I am sitting
in a carrel, inhaling breaths sixty-eight degrees cold,
trying to squeeze poetic images onto the pad
beneath my hand, as from an empty tube of paint.

If only I were a child, small and nimble, strong enough
to climb through the window into the sheltering hollow
where the tree's branches merge, and nestle there,
amid ferns growing like satin whiskers along the limbs.
Then – I would be the poem, and all the solemn,
silenced adults at their desks behind the glass would feel
embarrassed to be staring at me, unsure that I was real.

MY SMART SCARF

Bound for some chic luncheon spot
in Belgravia, it simply slipped away,
absconded like a child, dazzled
by sights and faces on the bright red
double-decker bus. I missed it
not immediately enough, then
fiercely, for the harmony it stripped
from skirt and blouse and shoes. And
something in its absence made me ache
for home, and worry at the loosening
of knots a trip away can bring.

When you telephoned last night,
I wondered that you didn't care
what streets I'd walked, or how
the Hyde Park daffodils are bursting.
I'd want to know each place you went,
the toothy English faces you had seen.
I miss you less when I can paint a picture
of your whereabouts, like my smart scarf
which I fancy now tucked snug
inside some poor woman's coat,
beyond mere adornment, comforting her
against the cold wind, making
her unfamiliar scent its own.

THE LITTLE LOSSES

It's Independence Day, and all
our small belongings
are claiming theirs.
I think it's willful, even diabolical,
the way they play at hide and seek –
my husband's wallet loves
to slip between the driver's seat
and door, often just before
he's amassed those masculine essentials
at the hardware store, inching through
a checkout line ten husbands deep.

My glasses, all eight pairs
placed with foresight
next to chairs about the house,
remove themselves at will.
I thought I might outsmart
the cell-phone charging cord
by buying two, but soon
the coily one went missing.
No doubt it has wriggled up
beneath an armchair and wound
itself contentedly among the springs,
like a baby anaconda.
The other disappeared a week ago,
leaving the phone bleating
like an orphaned lamb,
then surfaced in my makeup bag.

I often wonder whether
all those things that choose

to go astray see themselves
as signposts, gentling us
along a path toward
the keener pain
of deeper deprivations –
of the money we thought we saved,
our eyesight, or even
someone's whispered name.
And when I wonder this,
I bless the little losses
for their size.

IV. FLIGHT PLAN

BROODING

Fat blue spruce
beside my window,
spring-thickened,
concealing space
for nest-nestling –
a busy place
for cardinals.

Two chicks, two
gaping, beckoning
beaks, scrawn
of neck above
down-dusted
wings, all angle
and fold
parchment-spanned,
origami birds
but for need.

Father, red-robed
vigilance
lighting on a chair,
tail-feathers fanning,
paternity a-pulse –
peril-beacon,
protector.

Mother, unflagging
worm-courier
surreptitious,

settling her
dun-brown
feather-breasted
warmth amid
the satiated nest.

Oh, for feathered
instinct, unfettered
by the mind –
for knowing how
to nurture, what
to give, and when
to simply nestle
with the brood.

A WOMAN'S WORK

On the pink brick terrace
of our first home our firstborn
spends the afternoon
filling her plastic pail
on one side of her inflated
pool, then turns and tips it
'til water spills out
on the other side. Life
is work, and when her
work is done, and the last
of the necessary pailfuls
empty, she crawls over
the pool's bulging
top ring and wobbles
toward me through the sun,
glances back and frowns,
returns and stoops
to pick her careless,
dripping footprints up.

FLIGHT PLAN

Softly from the hemlock falls
a feathered ball of blue into
my sun-flecked yard.
Stunned it lies, unknown – unknowing –
then fluffs itself into a baby jay
and hops around, as though
the plunge weren't gravity's idea,
and finds a makeshift tree –
a cedar chair with slat-spanned legs
and solid seat to offer shelter from above.
Within, the fledgling bobs from slat to ground
to slat again, until its feathers
thrust outward into wings,
and then it flies the span.

Such relentless work goes not unnoticed –
now and then mother bird swoops down
with morsels to be proffered beak to beak,
then sails back up the tree and caws
a plaintive parental cry
about her errant child.
She has other work to do –
five more feathered forms
now fill the upper boughs with hops
and flutterings and make
the hemlock branches dance.

All spring the parent birds
had swooped in with bits

of debris as they built their home
then nested. But by the end of today
every chick has learned to fly
and flown away, and now – so suddenly –
the lively limbs are barren once again.

COMING OUT

for Alexa

It's National Coming Out Week –
as though the calendar could
summon reluctant birds to fly
in unison, like migrant geese.

When I was your age, coming out
meant white-frocked debutantes, flocks
set free from boarding school
as from a dovecote, fluttering
gaily into society.

Now coming out takes courage.
Praise to you, my fledgling,
who dared the changing winds
so early, an eaglet slipping
from the aerie into flight, knowing
how your wings were made to fly.

BIRTH BOND

for Nichol and Teddy

From the beginning,
warm slosh and pulsing
mother-heart, the bump
and tumble of womb-mate
and then, the rude world.

Disjoined by birth,
distinct names, weights,
then five days sundered
in separate isolettes,
a maze of tubes.

The slow, sweet teaching
of the breast. And sleep.
The gentling of hands,
heating lamps to help
their tiny organs thrive.

Strength enough now
to share a crib. Laid down
apart, they inch closer, 'til
touching heads,
mingling soft breaths.

BOTH WORLDS

The freckled gold of dawn-light
dances on the river's satin skin,
stirred by breezes faintly
whispering, breathing soft caress
onto the vast cool flow. I linger,
stretched out nude at water's lip,
fingering crisp lichens from the sun-warmed
swimming rock, flicking gray-green flakes
onto the water, tickling its surface.

Though years ago I plunged
with sensual abandon as my daughters do,
I savor now the sweet, seductive moments,
waiting for the primal urge to overwhelm.
I slide into the river, enfolded in its grace,
my eyes and mouth drinking in the air,
my body fathoming the world below,
each part curious, alive,
embraced by separate realms.

AS THE AFTERNOON SUN
DANCES ON THE RIVER

three sisters, naked,
of a certain age
as the French would say
step gingerly
down the sloping rock face
into the welcoming water –
bathers in a *tableau vivant*
suggestive of Cézanne.

Once
we would have leapt
from the swimming rock,
yelping at the cold,
our heads thrusting
through the surface; now
our sags and wrinkles
settle gently into the water,
where we paddle around
in small circles, necks
craning to keep our hair dry
before dinner, laughing
at what we have become,
so much the same way
our mother used to be.

IN STORAGE

Our lives are boxed up, sealed
with thick, transparent tape,
and labeled in large block letters
KITCHEN, LIVING ROOM,
as though the destinations
were a somewhere.

Yet here the cartons lie
in warehouse limbo, waiting
for a home. Back from Florida
for a week of work, dispossessed
of our northern furnished rental
for just one winter month,
we have unwrapped a mattress,
laid it on its box spring on the floor,
and closed our eyes each night,
the phantom rooms ordered
around us in imagination,
a kitchen bright with plants
and hanging copper pots,
our favorite green leather chairs
cozy by a brickwork fireplace,
the dogs curled on their pillows at our feet.

THE OLD SOLDIERS

They arrived like a ragtag army –
forty-two cartons of books to billet
in my home – bequest from Lili, eccentric
godmother. Dog-eared and dusty, they
settled into shelves built hastily along
our basement walls, claimed pride
of place as I settled them in ranks –
Vonnegut and Thurber, Gertrude Stein
and cookbooks, travelogues and tracts
by Thirties socialists, whose revolutions
have long since played out. Ranks
of Churchill histories, primers for
a generation. No strangers, these tomes.
I had followed them, as the clipped-out
book reviews spilling from inside their covers
grew yellow over time: from New York shelves
to Rome and back again to Cambridge, had
borrowed them, discussed them over decades
of red wine, deep into the night, as Lili probed
my mind, from teen years onward, for depths.
Lili, who wore only black and white, and
never talked about her past.

And now they must move on, again.
Where we're going to live, there is no room.
That they have been loved, makes them
unwanted. Unjacketed and faded, even
the Five College Book Sale turned them
away, would have consigned them to
the terrible heaping dumpster. I took them
home, resettled them on shelves. Brought in

book dealers, watched them shake their heads,
listened to one say I should just
throw them out – "They're only books," he said.
And so they are, old veterans. Yet
I can honor them with one last purpose:
they will bring warmth, for I shall
cremate them, one by one, over long
winter evenings, at my hearth.

BENEDICTION

Out of morning mist
a doe appears
wide-eyed and tawny,
on the neighbor's lawn,
dazed to find herself
so far from woods
on rich green
summer carpeting.
She grazes, looks up,
wanders off,
planting delicate hooves
upon the dew.

So it has been,
with our every move –
parting with an old home,
settling in anew –
within a week, always,
deer – one, or two, once
a herd of five sprinting
down the street. How
could they know? Or
do we seek them,
only as we move,
almost as a blessing?

V. ECLIPSE

THE WATER SNAKE

I saw an enormous water snake
slink across my path,
and felt a chill
as she passed.

She wasn't quick.
She didn't seem to care
which way her torpid slither led.

Her skin was
like an ancient kettle
tarnished with soot,
with little flecks of brown
that caught the sun.

I admired her rapid tongue,
her clever tongue
which tasted
the air for insects
or danger.

Neither of us saw
the hired man
who had been raking leaves,
raise a birch log
then slam it
on her flat black head,
pinning her to the ground.

Her heavy body twisted,
jerked, writhed,

and then lay still.
The man stood,
grinning, toothless,
whispered "Watch this,"
snapped his jackknife open,
and slid the blade down
the snake's tawny underside.

A motion caught my eye.
Something thin and black
and squirming squeezed
through the gash, and
then another, and another, until
a dozen writhing baby snakes
had shimmied free and slithered
into the underbrush,
and the mother-form
lay emptied, like a
ragged leather purse.

ECLIPSE

You start the evening hour round
and bountiful, graciously bright,
adorned with features renowned,
a monthly crescendoing sight.

Then as the minutes pass, a shade
screens a side of your luminous sphere,
and slowly spreads its eerie fade
'til your glow has all but disappeared.

Oh, cruel moon, to dance into dark
with a pale red diaphanous veil,
to mimic life's ephemeral arc
and mock how we humans grow frail.

HER SEXTANT

for Lauren

Do you know the Down East fog
that can swallow up the rocky coast
in one quick bite? Once, cruising
through it, I marveled as our skipper
steered the boat, engines
thrumming at full throttle
with nothing but a blinking screen
as guide.

Just so, as though
possessed of some internal sonar
you always seemed to navigate
the swells and depths with ease,
slipping through the narrow channels
where your sisters had foundered
on a reef. We worried then, when
your swift ship rocked aimless
for a time, as though your guidance
system had failed – but you had only paused
to call on stars, bird-cry and buoy bell
before you journeyed on.

COTTON BAY

Cotton Bay lies in the embrace of reef
stretching aqua-clear across the water,
an easy reach from the wide smiling beach
to a teeming coral underworld where fish
fancifully wardrobed dart and dance
below my mask and snorkel. Deceived
by flippers and effortless suspension,
I think myself one of them, gliding
'til suddenly the reef plunges
to the ocean floor, and fear pricks
through my limbs that I will fall.

Fall, as I fell last night, dreaming
of a hat launched playfully through air,
and when I leapt to grasp it, frisbee-like
in flight, the unsuspected cliff gave way
ten thousand feet, and I was falling
to the mundane certainty of death.

What moment plants the seed of dreams
and fears? Perhaps it was that dear man
who greeted us for cocktails at his door
high on the ridge above the bay, hand thrust out
beneath his smile, bow tie askew, shoelaces
dangling. When he spoke, empty holes
lay gaping between remembered phrases,
"Nice to see you" – "Welcome" – "Come in" –
like airless space between the stars.

EATING OUT WITH BARBARA

Vail, Colorado

This year, her slender ribs and collarbone
press sharper ridges outward through the tight
fitted sweater, and her eyes look vastly larger than before.
She labors through the menu, choosing
carefully three appetizers, requesting substitutions,
wasabi for sage mayonnaise, mustard with her nori roll,
and Chardonnay, two glasses, which she will mete out
precisely, between each precious, peril-ridden bite –

> as though her mind's suspended
> in a bell jar, weighted
> with steel bars, descending
> every meal-time
> into the ocean depths,
> where primitive, primordial
> fishes press and scrape
> against her cage
> and great white sharks
> menace with hacksaw
> rows of teeth.
> The pressure as she descends
> is more than her transparent
> bubble can withstand.
> In the vast silence, her screams
> scream back at her, get swallowed
> in the vacuum, and still she falls…

"If she ever took communion,"
her husband jokes,
"she'd ask for Chardonnay,"
then changes the subject,
steering us through powder snow
to politics with practiced ease.
He has plowed her perilous sea
long enough to find safe harbor
for others, perhaps himself.

TRASH DAY

Pajama-clad, his slippers
parting pebbles into
an unkempt double wake,
our aging neighbor
must have gauged the distance
to the curb within his capability,
not considering the return.

His wife, now keeper, slept.
Can't a man be of some use?
To lug a weekly plastic bag
from house to street links
a man with neighbors, makes
a kind of brotherhood.

Proud of deed, he turned to will
his heavy feet toward home,
and fell, and lay, and waited.

Must it come to this,
that his rescuer, a man himself
past sixty, unfamiliar, should
heave him up and stagger with him
to the door? What did that
younger neighbor see? The eyes
of an animal, trapped
inside a body, seeking what?
Forgiveness. For the shame
of growing old.

AFTERMATH

              acrid
the air   hangs   still
swirls of ash
        settle   inch-thick
man and monument
to dust   returned

toppled towers   crumbling
          dreams
spawning   nightmares
            the city reels

wrap
        the offense
in   ten thousand
        acts of
                care
        of community

an oyster
        lapping   nacre
layer on layer
        around
            a grain of sand

LINK

Josh Rosenthal   unaccounted for
        among the thousands,
linked to me by   nothing   but
        a fragile business tie,
yet bound forever.

Each human figure
        leaping   screaming   flaming
wears his face.

LABOR

On a back street in Cambridge,
I see a woman lying on her side
atop the thickened matte of what was
once a lawn, her head propped
on one hand above her elbow,
wispy strands of gray hair slipping
from the bun at the back of her head
into a tousled ring around her face.
Only her free hand is moving, thumb
and forefinger, the gap between them
opening and closing rhythmically,
purposefully. A glint of sunlight
beneath her hand reveals a pair
of kitchen shears moving at a slow clip
through the unkempt blades of grass.
She lies by the front corner of the house,
a neatly cut five-foot-wide strip
of shorter growth along the side of it
stretching out behind her like a wake.
How much she has accomplished,
how much lies ahead! I think of pioneers
crossing unmapped lands, of Sisyphus
rolling a boulder uphill, of Hercules
cleaning those Augean stables in one day.

VI. LISTEN TO YOUR HEART

GYPSY SONG

San Miguel de Allende

He looks like an El Greco
come to life, black eyes
pools of sorrow, face longer
than the end of time. Yet when
the gypsy Xavier embraces
his guitar, it is as though
she were a woman loved,
awaiting his caress. Blunt
fingers of his left hand press
mournful chords into
her slender neck, while the long
nails of his other hand stroke
quivering strings, coaxing them to voice.
Of what do they sing?
El amor y la muerte, love
and death – is that not all there is?

LISTS

He decorates paper napkins, the backs
of envelopes and thank-you notes
with lists tossed from that fertile, untamed mind
like contents of his pockets at day's end
(quarters, Kleenex, floss, dimes, Swiss army knife
scattered helter-skelter on the bed) – lists
of taxes due, new dog collars, cleaning
to pick up, a tennis racquet to restring.

Always I search the lists for his secret
inner thoughts, imagine common words
as crumbs along the path to fathoming
his pathos, his questions of existence,
yet languish in the indecipherable code
of his unknowable masculine mystery.

LISTEN TO YOUR HEART

Last night I heard you
on the telephone
counseling our daughter,
about a man –
"Listen to your heart,"
you said, and I thought
about the doctor giving you
the same advice, how
you must have stepped
into the pharmacy to buy
the stethoscope, nonchalant,
as though it were a box
of bandaids, or aspirin,
and how that night, sitting
by the fireside, we listened
to your heart, galloping
across the prairie of your chest,
reining in to pause, then pivoting
and racing off again, the wind
picking up, the sky so leaden
you could taste the coming rain –
miles off, but bearing down.

IN FLORIDA, AFTER YOU LEFT

the tulips you'd arranged, grown
leggy as a clutch of sixth-grade girls,
shed petals, a discarded skirt around
their bowl. They lie there still,
amid pepperings of deep russet in slatted
sunlight, as I sprawl in my nightgown
on the couch. The fabric of our woven lives
shears away so quickly when
we're in separate places. I begin
to understand the recluse now, how
her stacks of fading newspapers build,
why she finds no need to open blinds,
or make the bed. This week alone
feels like a rehearsal for the day
one of us will not come back.
Do you think of it as practice, too?
At night, I actually miss the snores
that keep me awake.
The refrigerator's hum becomes a roar.
When my sister, twice a widow, phones,
asks "How's everything in the sunny south?"
I say how still the house seems, with
my husband gone. Softly she responds,
"Welcome to my world."

SUMMER LIGHTS

Last night I lit the lovely little lanterns
you'd planted improbably among
geranium beds along the terrace wall.
Dangling from slender, bending stems
they lilted like phosphorescent fantasies
in the evening breeze above the river, 'til
soon one faded, and then another failed.
I watched, dismayed. With easy grace,
you would have stepped inside the cottage
to your stash of votives and replaced them,
as simply as I would sew a missing button on.

A thousand times I've watched you tend
the candles or wash away splashed wax
from hurricane mantles to purify their gleam.
Candles are what you bring to us,
the good redeemed from childhood years
of Catholic obligations, and my assuming
your devotions feels quite wrong. And so
I sat there, taking in the growing darkness,
mulling over all the ways one person
can light another's life.

ABOUT THE AUTHOR

Deming Holleran has been writing poems for the past twenty years. Inspired by a poetry course at Dartmouth College taught by Phyllis Katz and Donald Sheehan, director of The Frost Place at the time, she wrote a collection of verse for her Masters thesis. With Phyllis, she founded an ongoing poetry workshop, the Still Puddle Poets. Thus began a joyful symbiosis with fellow poets in the Hanover, NH area and with The Frost Place, where she has attended many summer conferences and has served as board chair for five years.

Classmates at Harvard and married almost fifty years, Deming and her husband Romer are the parents of four daughters and eight grandchildren, and live with their two cockapoo pups in Lebanon, New Hampshire, and Vero Beach, Florida. Many of her poems are rooted in a family place on an island in the St. Lawrence River. An avid skier, tennis player and golfer, she continues to search for a way to integrate these passions into her poetry life.

This book is set in Garamond Premier Pro, which had its genesis in 1988 when type-designer Robert Slimbach visited the Plantin-Moretus Museum in Antwerp, Belgium, to study its collection of Claude Garamond's metal punches and typefaces. During the mid-fifteen hundreds, Garamond—a Parisian punch-cutter—produced a refined array of book types that combined an unprecedented degree of balance and elegance, for centuries standing as the pinnacle of beauty and practicality in type-founding. Slimbach has created an entirely new interpretation based on Garamond's designs and on compatible italics cut by Robert Granjon, Garamond's contemporary.

To order additional copies of this book
or other Antrim House titles, contact the publisher at

Antrim House
21 Goodrich Rd., Simsbury, CT 06070
860.217.0023, AntrimHouse@comcast.net
or the house website (www.AntrimHouseBooks.com).

•

On the house website
in addition to information on books
you will find sample poems, upcoming events,
and a "seminar room" featuring supplemental biography,
notes, images, poems, reviews, and
writing suggestions.